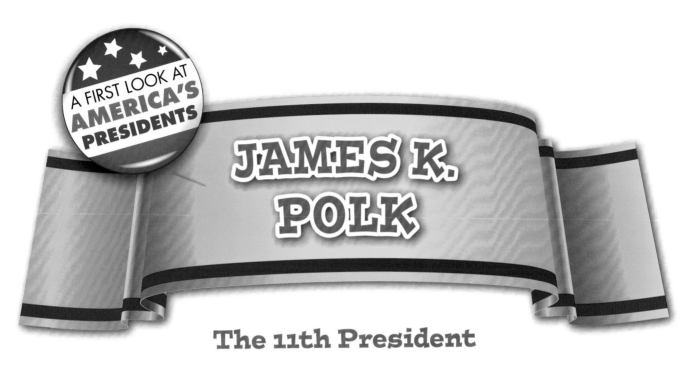

JAMES K. POLK

The 11th President

by Diane Bailey

Consultants:
Philip Nash, Associate Professor of History
Pennsylvania State University
Sharon, Pennsylvania

Soo Chun Lu, Associate Professor of History
Indiana University of Pennsylvania
Indiana, Pennsylvania

BEARPORT
PUBLISHING

New York, New York

Credits

Cover, Courtesy White House; 4, © North Wind Picture Archives/Alamy; 5, Courtesy National Portrait Gallery; 6, Courtesy James Polk Home and Museum/Wikimedia; 7T, Courtesy New England Journal of Medicine; 7B, © North Wind Picture Archives/Alamy; 8, Courtesy Executive Office of the President; 9T, Courtesy White House/Pete Souza; 9B, © Classic Image/Alamy; 10, Courtesy Library of Congress; 11T, © Jacobolus/Wikimedia; 11B, Courtesy U.S. Senate; 13, © David Gaudin/Dreamstime; 14, Courtesy Library of Congress; 15T, © Kevin Tietz/Dreamstime; 15B, © Americanspirit/Dreamstime; 17T, © Swan555/Dreamstime; 17B, © Classic Stock/Alamy; 17BR, © Mark Haughwout/Dreamstime; 18, Courtesy Dsmspence/Wikimedia; 19T, Courtesy Library of Congress (photo by Matthew Brady); 19B, © Americanspirit/Dreamstime; 20T, © Ffooter/Dreamstime; 20B, Courtesy Executive Office of the President; 21L, Courtesy Library of Congress; 21R, © Thomas Vieth/Dreamstime; 22, © Franck Fotos/Alamy.

Publisher: Kenn Goin
Editor: Jessica Rudolph
Creative Director: Spencer Brinker
Production and Photo Research: Shoreline Publishing Group LLC

Library of Congress Cataloging-in-Publication Data

Names: Bailey, Diane, 1966– author. | Nash, Philip, consultant.
Title: James K. Polk : the 11th president / by Diane Bailey ; consultant,
   Philip Nash, Associate Professor of History, Pennsylvania State University.
Description: New York, New York : Bearport Publishing, [2017] | Series: A
   first look at America's Presidents | Includes bibliographical references
   and index. | Audience: Ages 6–10._
Identifiers: LCCN 2016012112 (print) | LCCN 2016012628 (ebook) | ISBN
   9781944102661 (library binding) | ISBN 9781944997335 (ebook)
Subjects: LCSH: Polk, James K. (James Knox), 1795–1849—Juvenile literature.
   | Presidents—United States—Biography—Juvenile literature.
Classification: LCC E417 .B165 2017 (print) | LCC E417 (ebook) | DDC
   973.6/1092—dc23
LC record available at http://lccn.loc.gov/2016012112

For more information, write to Bearport Publishing Company, Inc., 45 West 21st Street, Suite 3B, New York, New York 10010. Printed in the United States of America.

10 9 8 7 6 5 4 3 2 1

CONTENTS

A Growing Nation

James K. Polk was a powerful leader. As president, he set big goals and worked hard to meet them. His biggest goal was to help the country **expand**. Because of Polk, the United States became a bigger, stronger nation.

When Polk was president, many Americans moved to new lands in the West.

James K. Polk was the 11th president. He served from 1845 to 1849.

A Tough Childhood

James Knox Polk was born in 1795 in North Carolina. As a boy, he was often too sick to go to school, so he studied at home. At age 16, James had an **operation** on his stomach to improve his health. Soon after, he was able to go to college. Then he became a lawyer.

When James was ten, his family moved to this house in Tennessee.

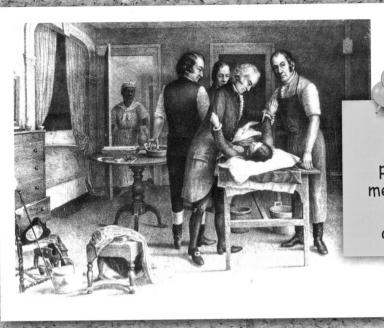

In the early 1800s, operations were very painful. There were no medicines to put patients to sleep. They were awake the whole time!

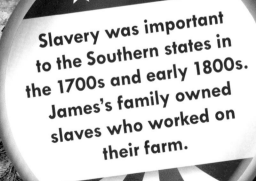

Slavery was important to the Southern states in the 1700s and early 1800s. James's family owned slaves who worked on their farm.

7

Talking Things Out

As a young man, Polk became interested in politics. In 1825, the people of Tennessee voted him into **Congress**. Lawmakers in Congress argued about whether slavery should be outlawed. Some people lost their tempers, but not Polk. He tried to help everyone talk things through.

Some arguments in Congress led to fights!

In 1824, Polk married Sarah Childress.

Polk served as Speaker of the House from 1835 to 1839. The Speaker is in charge of the House of Representatives, which is part of Congress.

Running for President

In 1844, Polk ran for president. Not many Americans knew who he was, but he had good ideas. He promised to add more land to the United States. A lot of voters liked that idea. It was a close race, but Polk won.

Polk ran for president in 1844, with George Dallas (right) as his vice president.

In 1844, the United States was much smaller than it is today, and had only 26 states.

In the 1800s, many Americans believed it was right for the country to expand west from the Atlantic Ocean to the Pacific Ocean. This idea is called manifest destiny.

Polk ran for president against Henry Clay (left), who was a popular politician. Many people thought Clay would win the race.

Into Oregon

In the 1840s, many Americans moved west to an area called Oregon Country. People from Great Britain had also settled there. Both America and Britain wanted to own the land. President Polk worked out a solution to avoid war. In 1846, the two countries signed a **treaty** to divide the land.

People traveled to the northwestern United States on the Oregon Trail.

Land added to the United States after the Oregon Treaty of 1846

Modern state borders

Oregon Trail

Washington

Montana

Oregon

Idaho

Wyoming

California

Nevada

Utah

N W E S

A farm in Oregon

The journey on the Oregon Trail was long and dangerous. People took the risk because they wanted land to build homes and farms.

Going to War

Polk looked for other ways to help the nation grow. In 1846, America and Mexico argued about where the border between Mexico and Texas should be. Polk believed some of the land claimed by Mexico should be part of Texas. He also wanted much of Mexico's western lands. That year, the two countries went to war.

American soldiers attack a fort in Mexico during the Mexican-American War.

Texas was once part of Mexico. In 1836, Texas won its freedom from Mexico. Texas was its own country until 1845, when it became part of the United States.

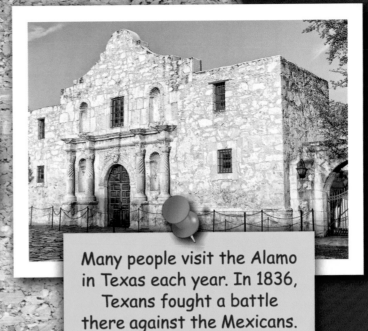

Many people visit the Alamo in Texas each year. In 1836, Texans fought a battle there against the Mexicans.

This was the flag of Texas when it was a free country. Today, it's the flag of the state of Texas.

Fighting for Land

Polk took charge of the war. He planned battles and gave orders to military leaders. After two years, the United States won. Mexico was forced to sell much of its land to America.

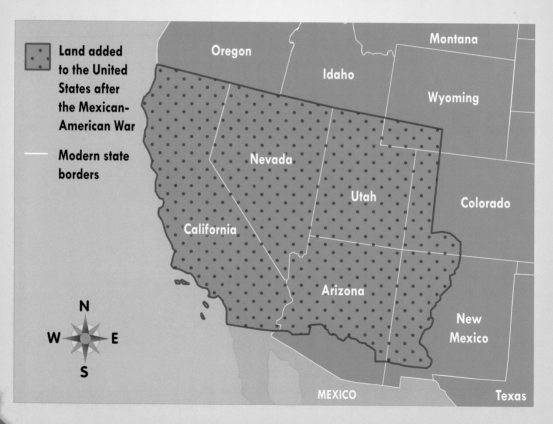

Legend:
- Land added to the United States after the Mexican-American War
- Modern state borders

Oregon, Idaho, Montana, Wyoming, Nevada, Utah, California, Colorado, Arizona, New Mexico, MEXICO, Texas

The West has many natural resources. Just before the Mexican-American War ended, gold was found in California. Many Americans moved there to try to strike it rich.

People looked for gold in rivers using shovels and pans.

17

A Strong Leader

President Polk left office in 1849. Today, Polk is remembered for being a strong leader. He helped add about 1.2 million square miles (3.1 million sq km) to the United States. The land in the West gave Americans new places to build farms and cities.

Polk County, in Iowa, is just one of many places named after the 11th president.

Polk never took a vacation when he was president. This may have led to poor health and his death at age 53, three months after leaving office.

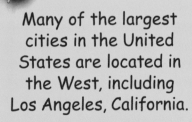

Many of the largest cities in the United States are located in the West, including Los Angeles, California.

TIMELINE

Here are some major events from James K. Polk's life.

1795
James K. Polk is born in Mecklenburg County, North Carolina.

1818
Polk graduates from the University of North Carolina.

1800

1810

1820

1824
Polk marries Sarah Childress.

1846–1848
The Mexican-American War is fought.

1825–1839
Polk serves in the U.S. House of Representatives.

1844
Polk is elected president.

1830

1840

1850

1839–1841
Polk serves as governor of Tennessee.

1849
Polk dies soon after leaving office.

1846
The Oregon Treaty adds land to the northwestern United States.

FACTS and QUOTES

Polk was the oldest of ten children.

Polk did not trust banks. He hid all his money in paper bags in his house.

Polk's nickname was "Young Hickory" because he was a lot like his friend, President Andrew Jackson. Jackson was called "Old Hickory."

"I am the hardest working man in this country."

"Peace, plenty, and contentment reign [rule] throughout our borders."

GLOSSARY

Congress (KON-gress) one of the three branches of the U.S. government; it includes the U.S. Senate and the U.S. House of Representatives

expand (eks-PAND) to increase in size

manifest destiny (MAN-ih-fest DESS-tih-nee) the belief that the United States should expand from the Atlantic to the Pacific coasts

natural resources (NACH-ur-uhl REE-sorss-iz) materials found in nature, such as trees, water, and gold, that are useful to people

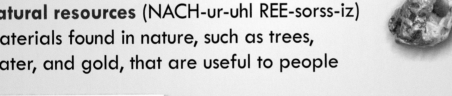

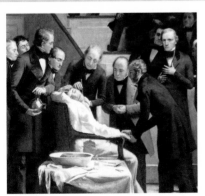

operation (*ah*-pur-AY-shun) a procedure that a doctor performs on a person's body to restore health

treaty (TREE-tee) an agreement in writing between nations

Index

Read More

Gaines, Ann Graham.
*James K. Polk: Our Eleventh
President.* North Mankato,
MN: Child's World (2008).

Rumsch, BreAnn. *James
K. Polk: 11th President of
the United States.* Edina,
MN: ABDO (2009).

Venezia, Mike. *James K.
Polk: Eleventh President
1845–1849.* New York:
Chldren's Press (2005).

Learn More Online

To learn more about James K. Polk, visit
www.bearportpublishing.com/AmericasPresidents

About the Author:
Diane Bailey has
written dozens
of books for kids.
She lives in Kansas.

24